To George & Jean Westers —
Hope you enjoy my
pictures —
Don Dailey

Kind regards,
Susan Kuhnke

ROCHESTER
City and Countryside

Photography • David Wesley
Text • Ivan Kubista
Design • Bruce Holter
Production • Farinacci & Associates Inc.
Laser color separations • Color House
printing • John Roberts Co.

Published by FarWes Publications, St. Paul, Minnesota

International Standard Book Number 0-9603182-0-8

ROCHESTER
City and Countryside

PHOTOGRAPHY
BY DAVE WESLEY

TEXT
BY IVAN KUBISTA

It is a temptation, in editing a book about Rochester, to concentrate on the historical influence of the Mayo family in establishing the city as a world-famous medical center. It is, in fact, difficult to do otherwise because the words, "Rochester," and "Mayo Clinic" have become inseparable in the minds of untold millions all over the planet. Nevertheless, there is a city of Rochester, Minnesota that exists beyond the illustrious walls of the clinic buildings — a modern, progressive city with social, cultural, recreational and industrial characteristics often obscured by the medical renown. It is the purpose of this book to present these other faces of Rochester, and to familiarize the reader with the rich heritage of the region which provides its existence. For those desiring a more detailed account of the medical growth of Rochester, we heartily encourage a reading of Helen Clapesattle's classic work, "The Doctors Mayo." Through this volume we hope to instill a greater appreciation for Rochester and its environs by helping the visitor . . . be he clinic patient or vacationing tourist . . . discover the delights of a truly unique region.

Southeast Minnesota is so distinctively different from the rest of the state — in its topography, its climate, the character of its villages and towns — that it is almost a little state unto itself. And if one looks at the area with that in mind, then the capital would have to be Rochester, its largest city.

And as southeast Minnesota differs, so Rochester differs remarkably from other major cities in the state. Its unique development has, in fact, made it one of the most famous cities in the United States if not in the world.

The most obvious contributor to this position, of course, is Rochester's reputation as a healing mecca. The Mayo Clinic is the largest association of privately practicing physicians on earth, a group many believe represents the highest refinement of medical diagnosis and treatment.

Rochester's visitors, therefore, include people from all parts of the globe. Of the half million who flock to the city each year, at least half seek the services of the Mayo Clinic.

The number of clinic patients is astounding. But so is the fact that there are still about 250,000 people who come to Rochester for other reasons. Considering its comparatively modest size of about 60,000, one must assume its attraction goes well beyond its fame as a medical center. And so it does.

But to fully understand this attraction, one must go beyond the city limits and observe the character of its environs, the region in which it sprouted and over which it exerts such economic influence.

In many ways southeast Minnesota resembles an area one might encounter in the pages of a forgotten childrens' book. A place where shady forests blanket rolling hills and meadows; where tidy farms, with chubby red barns and softly spinning windmills, are tucked away in little valleys; where chuckling trout streams meander lazily through the woodlands, occasionally venturing out through sunsplashed pastures trod by fat, contented cattle.

It is a place where agriculture still maintains a firm grip; where tiny villages and hamlets have grown no larger than is necessary to serve their immediate rural clients; where corn and the dairy cow remain the staple economy.

It is, in short, the kind of place most often envisioned by those who long for a "home in the country." This may at least partially explain why rural communities here still thrive while those in other areas of the country have waned as population shifts to the larger cities.

Most area residents freely admit that while they might fare better economically elsewhere, they prefer the non-monetary values nature has so abundantly bestowed on this corner of Minnesota.

Minnesota at large is associated with its fabled ten thousand lakes (there are actually about 15,000), but southeast Minnesota is characterized by its beautiful rivers and streams. The most gorgeous of these is the Root River, a scenic waterway which begins its flow south of Rochester and winds through a lush valley toward the Mississippi.

About 35 miles south of Rochester, U.S. Highway 16 begins to tag along the river, hugging the forested limestone bluffs as it connects numerous small towns.

Lanesboro, Preston, Rushford, Houston, Hokah and LaCrescent are all interesting river communities, each having a distinct character contributing to the peculiar flavor of the region. But the main highway routes indicate only a portion of that flavor. In between, on less traveled county and township roads, are the little hamlets and hidden valleys that fairly shout to be discovered. The names alone provoke curiosity — Pilot Mound, Money Creek, Tawny, Black Hammer and others. Every turn of the road in the maze of hills and coulees offers a new experience.

North of Rochester runs the Zumbro River, the main stem of which flows through the city itself. It has not the majestic, somewhat wild beauty of the Root, but contents itself as a more leisurely stream curling through dense woodlands and sleepy villages. The best inspection of the Zumbro River Valley is from the secondary roads running between villages such as Hammond, Mazeppa, Zumbro Falls and others.

It is to this kind of land that United States surveyors came in 1854 to plat town sites and encourage settlement in what was then the American frontier. Only three years before, a treaty had been negotiated with the Sioux Indians opening the entire southern part of Minnesota Territory to white settlement.

George Head

One of the town sites was staked out along the picturesque Zumbro River and, in that same year, had its first permanent settler, George Head. Head recognized the town's potential as an oasis for hordes of pioneers on their way from the east to the rich agricultural lands westward.

Whether it was out of his genuine love for his home town in New York State or from a lack of imagination is unknown, but Head called his new town Rochester. By the time Rochester was officially incorporated four years later, its population had grown to more than 1,400.

Such rapid growth was not uncommon among pioneer communities, and Rochester's situation at the time was not particularly noteworthy. Other towns were growing as quickly and, for a time at least, two appeared more promising than Rochester. These were Mantorville and Wasioja about 15 miles to the west.

But the great determiner of town fortunes in the 19th century was the railroad. When an east-west rail line was built in 1865 it bypassed those communities to run further south — directly through Rochester. From that moment Rochester's prospects were assured.

With the railroad came construction of a grain elevator and the city, little more than a decade old, quickly became the central depot for wheat being grown throughout southern Minnesota. Like the booming cattle towns that were to emerge in the western plains, Rochester suddenly found itself an indispensable trade center for an area encompassing hundreds of square miles.

But even before the railroad bestowed its blessings on the city, something equally important had occurred. In 1863, during the darkest year of the Civil War, Rochester was selected as headquarters for the enrollment board of the First Minnesota District. The board was in charge of enlistments and conscriptions for the Union Army and the district included all of southern Minnesota. The examining surgeon for this board was Doctor William Worrall Mayo who had been practicing in Le Sueur, a tiny settlement about 85 miles west.

Doctor Mayo served in this official capacity in Rochester until the war's end in 1865. Then, instead of returning to his home town, he built a cottage in Rochester and moved his family there as permanent residents.

The cottage no longer stands, but in its place is the imposing, grey-marbled clinic building bearing the Mayo name.

Rochester has always enjoyed a steady growth in population, but despite the importance of the Mayo Clinic, the number of permanent residents was still less than 30,000 in 1950 and the local economy rested primarily with services associated with the clinic and a retail trade supported by tens of thousands of transients each year. But only ten years later the number had grown by an astonishing 36 per cent to more than 40,500. By 1970 the figure increased to just under 54,000 — a jump of about 26% — with 1980 projections at about 70,000. These dramatic figures seem solid confirmation of Doctor William Worrall Mayo's early admonitions to expand and diversify community activities. In his day, Rochester owed its existence to "King Wheat" and the railroad and any decline in those areas was immediately reflected in the local economic picture.

Although the Mayo Clinic provided Rochester with a more enduring economy, it is doubtful the city would have grown at its present rate without the presence of a substantial industrial base. This was provided in 1956 when International Business Machines (IBM) chose Rochester as the site for a huge manufacturing complex. Employment at IBM was about 4,000 — as much as the Clinic itself — and ushered in a new era of growth.

Today Rochester has over 70 manufacturing firms employing about 7,000 people and a combined payroll exceeding $50

Towering above the hardwoods are the buildings of the Mayo Clinic. In their shadow is Rochester — a vibrant city of 70,000 and a social, cultural and economic phenomenon.

million. With manufacturing, of course, has grown a huge wholesale and retail trade accounting for a fourth of the city's total employment. As a retail trade center, Rochester serves an unusually large area extending as far as northern Iowa and western Wisconsin and with an estimated population of over 400,000.

Such a position is, of course, self-perpetuating in the favorable climate it creates for even more new industries and businesses. Indeed, Rochester appears as a perpetual "boom town" whose prospects appear undiminished in any forseeable future.

Doctor William Worrall Mayo's contributions to Rochester were not only in the field of medicine. He was an active politician who plunged into community life with as much zeal as he attacked the problems of healing. As an influential school board member he was largely responsible for Rochester's building of what was, at the time, the largest and most costly school in Minnesota.

As Rochester's mayor, and later as alderman, Doctor Mayo continuously urged the city council to make improvements that would lift the city from frontier town status. Largely as a result of his incessant urging, Rochester built its water system, a gas plant, its own electric power facility and a sewer system.

Always running for some office or other, Mayo lost two very close elections for the State Legislature before finally becoming a state senator in 1890.

Apprehensive of declining wheat prices in the 1870's, he urged Rochester to broaden its economic base to avoid dependence on a single commodity. He also fought on behalf of the farmers for better prices and better wheat grading procedures. Mayo himself bought a small farm in 1875 and took an active interest in livestock breeding and farm mechanization.

Of paramount importance, however, was his open-minded and scientific approach to medicine, a practice he imparted to his two sons, William and Charles. The two boys also became doctors and were known affectionately to the local citizens as "Doctor Will" and "Doctor Charlie."

A busy 19th century Rochester only three decades old.
This memorial to Doctor William Worrall Mayo fittingly portrays
him in an attitude of accomplishment — a pioneer in medicine as
well as community life.

Left, the famous Mayo brothers, Doctors Charles H. and William J. Mayo.
This office was Doctor Mayo's clearing house for new information leading to improved medical treatment.
This red brick building housed the original clinic before Dr. Henry Plummer convinced the Mayos that it was inadequate for their swelling number of patients.

Despite Rochester's early emergence as a major city, it had no hospital. Nor was there much incentive to build one until a tragic day in 1883.

On August 21 of that year a tornado struck with devastating force. Nearly all of Rochester suffered some damage, but the entire north end was demolished. Thirty-one lives were lost and hundreds injured in the deadly storm. With help from the Sisters of St. Francis, Doctor Mayo and his sons fabricated makeshift hospital quarters in a local dance hall and in the convent.

The catastrophe prompted the Sisters of St. Francis to build and operate a permanent hospital, a project which was realized six years later when St. Mary's hospital opened its doors. The Mayos took charge of its operations and, with a proper facility, Rochester's medical reputation began to grow. Gradually the Mayo doctors, working with other physicians as a private group, evolved what was known as the Mayo Clinic by the turn of the century.

Today St. Mary's, with 1000 beds, is the world's largest private hospital.
Sharing the present need for hospital space now is the Rochester Methodist Hospital, completed in 1966. Clinic patients requiring hospitalization are sent to either of the two.

In addition to these famous institutions, Rochester has the Olmsted Community Hospital which provides facilities for general practitioners. Also, the State Hospital, established as a mental care center in 1879, provides exceptionally advanced programs of treatment to round out Rochester's role as a healing center for both physical and mental disorders.

Entrance to St. Mary's Hospital, Rochester, the largest private
hospital in the World.

Rochester's parks and natural areas cater to human needs in a
technology-oriented world.

The new Mayo Clinic Building, completed in 1954

A typical exhibit at the Olmsted County Historical Museum, one of Minnesota's finest. Below: some of the famous geese that make Rochester their home year around.

The city of Rochester maintains two dozen parks which provide the nucleus for a wide range of recreational activity. A favorite is Mayo Park with its formal gardens and sculptured memorials to the famous doctors. Its scenic grounds, with the sparkling Zumbro River winding through, provide a backdrop for many summer events including an annual Festival of the Arts.

Another favorite area is Silver Lake Park, a short distance northwest of the downtown area. Twenty thousand wild Canadian geese winter here each year and many are year-around residents, raising their young and accepting handouts with quiet dignity. From time to time they take to the air and fill the sky with V-formations of various sizes. Rochester's geese have become one of the hallmarks of the city.

The scope of recreational opportunities in and around the area have given Rochester yet another image — that of a destination for vacationers. Thousands come each year to make Rochester their headquarters while they take in the historic sites, visit the art galleries, attend local concerts and stage performances, or pursue the more active sports of fishing, canoeing and golf.

Informative tours are always available of the famous hospitals, the larger industries and even of farming operations in the area. This, combined with the seemingly unlimited variety of restaurants, night clubs and shops, has made Rochester a vacation area in itself rather than a stopover for travellers going elsewhere.

It is only natural, then, that Rochester is headquarters for Hiawathaland — the twelve counties of southeast Minnesota organized to promote tourism in the area. The name is derived from the Mississippi Valley — popularly called the Hiawatha Valley — which forms the eastern border of Hiawathaland, and which once served as home for the Sioux tribes.

Indeed, there is so much of interest within a mere hour's drive in any direction from the city that any attempt to see it all during one trip may be an exercise in frustration. Rochester is part of such a unique region that it becomes worthwhile to explore at least some of the countryside beyond the city limits.

Lodging and restaurant facilities abound in a city which claims
6000 visitors at any given moment.

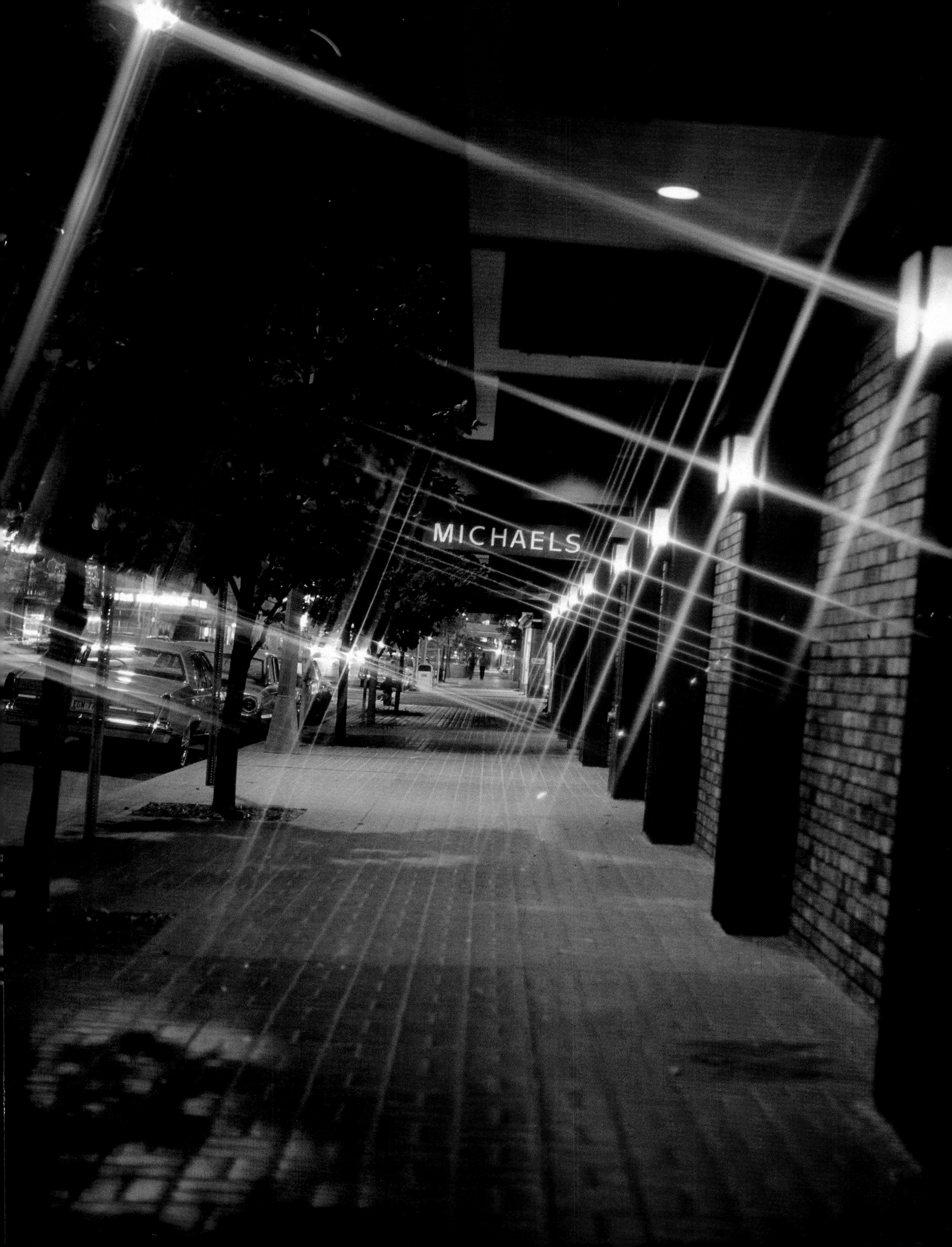
MICHAELS

Dragons, heads and mythical birds adorn the Plummer Building,
which housed the Mayo Clinic until 1954.
Terra cotta figures, molded in many pieces and carefully sealed
together; ornate windows and sculpted doors — all are perennial
grist for artists and photographers.

The Plummer Building, which once housed the entire Mayo
Clinic, is named for Doctor Henry Plummer, who joined the
Mayo partnership in 1901 and whose work is often ranked in
importance along with that of the Mayos themselves. Besides his
gifts as a medical doctor, Plummer was endowed with
extraordinary abilities in organization and in applying the latest
scientific technologies to his practice. The emergence of the
Mayo Clinic as such is directly due to his convincing the Mayos
that medical specialization can work only if a group of specialists
function as a unit with regard to the patient.

The Carillon

Visitors strolling the streets of downtown Rochester may wonder where the captivating music comes from. They need only look to the tower atop the Plummer Building, where a 56-bell carillon strikes up regular concerts.

The bells are a direct result of Doctor William J. Mayo's fascination with carillons while in England. When the Plummer Building — which once was the main housing for the Mayo Clinic — was under construction about 1925, there were no plans for the tower. With Doctor Mayo's urging, however, the blueprints were revised and a proper addition made for the bells.

In 1928 the original carillon — 23 bronze bells cast in an English foundry — was installed as a gift from Doctors Will and Charlie. In 1977 thirty-three new bells were added to give the carillon a four and one-half octave range, making it one of the most complete in North America.

Carillon concerts are scheduled regularly during the week, and on holidays and special occasions, and last from 20-25 minutes. The performer enjoys the title of Bellmaster and plays the carillon by pressing levers arranged much like a piano keyboard. The levers, in turn, pull wires attached to the clappers in corresponding bells. Rochester's present Bellmaster is Dean Robinson, who has held the post since 1958.

The original Bellmaster was the late James Drummond and he performed on the carillon for three decades. He described his job during that period as giving "peace and inspiration and a lift of the spirit to Rochester visitors, which was the intent of the carillon's donors, the Brothers Mayo."

Far left - Reflected by a clinic windowpane, these bronzed
copper figures of bicyclists represent Man and Recreation
Below - A bronze figure representing Man and Freedom

The Mayo Clinic Building, built in 1954, is primarily a functional structure — yet its designers knew the importance of providing a positive atmosphere for those who would use it. A major element in creating a proper environment was the inclusion of art — not just for the sake of art but to give the otherwise forbidding building a personality; more than that, it would be art that reminded people of their own humanity and encourage them in at least a subliminal way.

The striking sculptures suspended on the building's exterior are the result of one of these art programs. Each the work of a different artist, the figures collectively portray Man in all important phases of his life.

On the north facade is a bronze figure representing Man and Freedom, a beautiful statement of the search for fulfillment and dignity. It was created by Ivan Mestrovic, a Yugoslav artist who himself spent half his life in that very quest. Before he began work on this particular piece he said ". . . it must be a sculpture important for its artistic expression. To all living beings, and in the first place to man, as the highest among them, individual freedom is the most precious, and to men of thought, freedom in general is as precious."

The four bronze figures mounted on the east face of the clinic (Page 28), are the careful work of William Zorach, a Lithuanian-born artist who became a major American sculptor before his death in 1966. The figures are titled Man and Achievement, and are designed to carry the viewer's eye continuously from one to the other. The upper left figure represents the thinker or philosopher; the upper right, the workers and builders; the lower left, moral standards and concern for others; the lower right, the farmers and shippers of goods — note the man is gathering a net.

On the south facade are three groups of bronzed copper figures representing Man and Recreation (Page 29). The bicyclists represent refreshing physical activity; the center group suggests a joyful family, and the last group of three bathers symbolize the quiet, reflective joy of nature. The sculptures were created by Abbott Pattison, an American artist of great reknown whose works are found in important museums of most major cities.

27

Golden trees become part of the Rochester scene in autumn.

A Zumbro River dam provides a local fisherman a chance to use
his angling skill as well as his climbing technique.

Festivals and celebrations of all kinds characterize communities
in the Rochester area, whether it be an annual gopher bounty
day, a parade or a bean feed.

Any celebration worthy of its name must have a parade; these
are times when an open space on the curb becomes as valuable
as a theatre box seat.

Minnesota summers are filled with parades. Here are samples of two — Rushford's Frontier Days (left) and the Fourth of July parade in downtown Rochester.

Rochester itself provides a host of annual events, from the Zumbro Art Festival to an annual rodeo. These scenes remind one that Rochester was once a frontier town like many others.

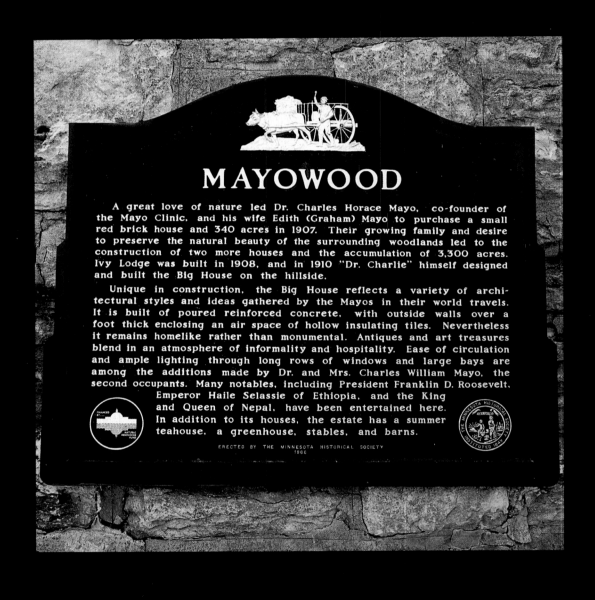

MAYOWOOD

A great love of nature led Dr. Charles Horace Mayo, co-founder of
the Mayo Clinic, and his wife Edith (Graham) Mayo to purchase a small
red brick house and 340 acres in 1907. Their growing family and desire
to preserve the natural beauty of the surrounding woodlands led to the
construction of two more houses and the accumulation of 3,300 acres.
Ivy Lodge was built in 1908, and in 1910 "Dr. Charlie" himself designed
and built the Big House on the hillside.

Unique in construction, the Big House reflects a variety of archi-
tectural styles and ideas gathered by the Mayos in their world travels.
It is built of poured reinforced concrete, with outside walls over a
foot thick enclosing an air space of hollow insulating tiles. Nevertheless
it remains homelike rather than monumental. Antiques and art treasures
blend in an atmosphere of informality and hospitality. Ease of circulation
and ample lighting through long rows of windows and large bays are
among the additions made by Dr. and Mrs. Charles William Mayo, the
second occupants. Many notables, including President Franklin D. Roosevelt,
Emperor Haile Selassie of Ethiopia, and the King
and Queen of Nepal, have been entertained here.
In addition to its houses, the estate has a summer
teahouse, a greenhouse, stables, and barns.

ERECTED BY THE MINNESOTA HISTORICAL SOCIETY
1968

Three generations of Mayo doctors occupying Mayowood
appear in this picture: Charles H. Mayo (right, his son Charles
W., and his grandson, Charles H. Mayo II.

41

Mayowood interiors — guests from the world over were once a
routine part of these settings.

The imposing residence of Doctor Henry Plummer. Completed
in 1924, it was eight years in the building. Until the first few
rooms were completed, the Plummers lived in a tent on the
grounds so that they could keep a watchful eye on construction.
The house is now Rochester city property.

The tower on the Plummer House grounds has become a
Rochester landmark.

Water-powered mills are still found in southeast Minnesota.
These quietly-neglected structures have become as much a part
of the landscape as the grass and flowers.

The primary modern function of covered bridges is to
. provide healthy doses of nostalgia. The bridge, below is in
Mantorville, the one on far right is in Zumbrota's city park. Both
are within a half-hour drive of Rochester.

West of Rochester is the village of Wasioja. Today it is hard to imagine this hamlet of 75 residents as being larger than Rochester at one time, but it, too, simmers with history.

In Wasioja is a Civil War Recruiting Station, the only one remaining in Minnesota. Nearby are the haunted ruins of a Baptist seminary. Perhaps the ruins are not unusual in themselves, but the story behind them is.

At the outbreak of the Civil War, ninety seminary students marched to the recruiting station to enlist, forming the nucleus of the Minnesota 2nd Regiment which saved the day at Chickamauga. None returned and the school closed. Fire destroyed the building in 1905.

From downtown Rochester Hiway 14 spans a century
in the twenty minute drive to Mantorville

Mantorville, thanks to the spirit of historic appreciation among its residents, has never been allowed to age beyond the mid-nineteenth century.

Thousands of years ago, when the mighty glaciers covered Minnesota, a few spots were left unmolested. The southeast corner is one of them. Journeying west from Rochester, however, the landscape begins to flatten in evidence of the leveling process of the glaciers during their last retreat. The scene becomes more prairie-like as opposed to the rough-and-tumble assortment of hills and valleys to the east. Rochester sits nearly on the glacial boundary line.

But if the westward area is wanting in scenery, compensation is more than made in the many places of interest. Among the better known of these is Mantorville, a village of 500 whose fame, like Rochester's, seems far out of proportion to its size.

Listed in the National Register of Historic Places, this village looks much as it did in the 19th century — which is only natural since many of its buildings and homes date from the 1860's! It is the seat of Dodge County and its courthouse has been in continuous use since 1865. Here too is the Hubbell House, one of Minnesota's oldest and most famous restaurants.

Once a prosperous hotel, the Hubbell House has been standing since 1857. During the 1862 Indian Uprising, local people flocked to the protection of its 40-inch thick limestone walls.

North and west of Mantorville is Wasioja, a village once bigger than Rochester. That was long ago, of course, when Wasioja had a population of 1,000 on an important Territorial Road stagecoach stop.

At that time it had a new seminary, a fairgrounds and racetrack, and many fine stores and buildings circled by limestone slab sidewalks cut from local quarries. Wasiojans enjoyed the weekly Wasioja Gazette (established in 1856) and looked forward to years of prosperity. But when a new railroad bypassed the town, those hopes were dashed and the community dwindled quickly until today only a few scattered homes and landmarks remain.

But what landmarks these are! Some are shown on pp. 52-53. At the historical museum in Mantorville is an elegant, old horsedrawn hearse with carved wooden tassels and fringed curtains at the windows. This was used in Wasioja until 1901. In front of Wasioja's old school building is a huge rock which wore out many pairs of trousers and shoes as children used it for a slide. The story goes that when parents threatened to remove the rock, the local cobbler said he'd have to close his shop and leave town. So the rock remains.

Top left - The Dodge county courthouse in Mantorville
Top right - Mantorville's famous boardwalk
Bottom - Mantorville's famous Hubbell House - now a restaurant,
it was originally a prominent hotel.

An ornate stained glass window of Mantorville's Hubbell House.

Legendary Lake Pepin, a widening of the Mississippi, is a fishing
haven and sailing spa an hour east of Rochester. It was here that
Ralph Samuelson invented the technique of water skiing in
1922.

MEIGHEN STORE

Horse medicine, school slates, eyeglasses, flour - all might
have been for sale or trade in the log cabin store opened in
1853 by Felix Meighen and Robert Foster boyhood friends from
Pennsylvania. As the only store in Fillmore County, it did a
thriving business and also served as a social center for the new
town of Forestville. The stagecoach station stood just behind the
store, and up the hill was the schoolhouse, located now by its
foundation ruins.

In 1856, Meighen and Foster built the present store, constructed
from the first brick made in the county. Although Foster with-
drew from the partnership in 1868, the Meighen family kept the
store open until 1910.

Some of the original trees still forest the Meighen homestead
area; the family set aside land about a mile past the store as a
park, and placed picnic tables for public use along the river bank.
The Meighen store, complete with its 1860 inventory of
merchandise, is now part of Forestville State Park, which
includes more than 3,000 acres.

South of Rochester, near the city of Preston, is one of
Minnesota's most unusual parks — Forestville State Park.
Named for a village now extinct, its chief attraction is the old
Meighan Store, out of business since 1910 but preserved now
by the State Historical Society.

Running straight east from Rochester is a well-known river, the Whitewater. Best known as a trout stream, the Whitewater flows through a state park by the same name, exactly twenty miles east of the city above the town of St. Charles.

Whitewater State Park is one of the most popular in the state protecting a lush section of the river valley which harbors much wildlife and native flora which can be observed along a carefully-planned system of nature trails.

Kellogg, another Mississippi River town, annually celebrates its
Melon Festival. What could be more refreshing on a hot
summer's day? These revelers demonstrate the idea with gusto.

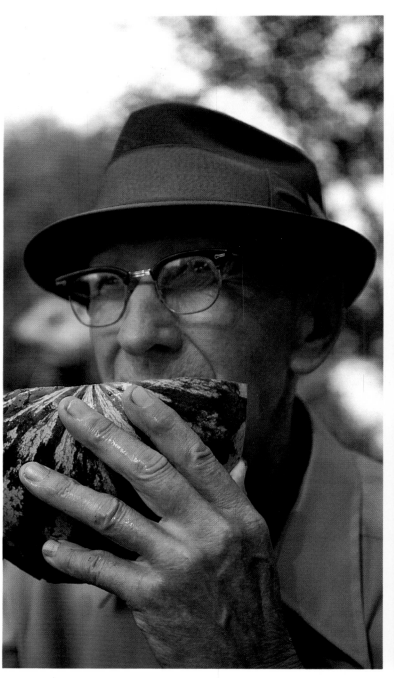

Rural southeast Minnesotans often categorize themselves as "hill dwellers" or "valley dwellers," with peculiar advantages for each. In winter, the valley dwellers enjoy less wind and warmer temperatures — but in summer a hill dweller enjoys cool breezes and vistas like the one shown here.

Those who live close to the land are conscious of close ties with their maker as well. The myriad churches of all denominations dotting rural southeast Minnesota bear this out.

Bursts of color in stain glass accents even the most
modest rural churches in an area where Sunday services
are still an integral part of life

Deserted classrooms of yesteryear, old schoolhouses are often the only nearby reminders that southeast Minnesota has changed since the turn of the century.
Some things never change, however . . . such as the perennial burst of wildflowers. Those at right bloom along Highway 52 just outside Rochester.

A little of the surrounding countryside manages a toehold in the
city. The weathervane is on a building located on Rochester's
Weather Hill.
This stone barn is only a few miles south of downtown
Rochester.

Round barns are an oddity anywhere, but southeast Minnesota
has several. This one, still used, is about 25 miles east of
Rochester near Troy.

White oak timbers, a favorite alternative to the limestone brick
used by early barn builders, make these seemingly brittle
structures as enduring as stone.
The land does not change but the means to work it does. But
whether sought with horse or tractor, the future is never further
away than the next rain.

Chopping hay for the silo . . . planting corn for the crib . . . the
bulk of field work here is directed toward feeding the dairy cows
which have long replaced King Wheat.

Some denizens of Rochester's rural environs: horses seeing
what is greener, geese on watch, and a nest of baby field mice
dozing in the sun.

Who knows why barns are red? For whatever reason, most of us
are glad that they are. This one near Zumbrota adds another hue
to nature's earthy color scheme.

The old barn and the wildflowers are commonplace in
Rochesters countryside. Below and at right are random samples
of the larger part of southeast Minnesota's population.

Armor-plated grasshoppers patrol the tall weeds beneath an
old barn. When the region was a wheat-growing capital, hordes
of these fellows posed a regular threat to the economy.

This area has a favorite saying: "when the fairies hang out their
wash to dry, it's a good day for making hay."
Death and life scenes played out in miniature among the
meadow grasses.

93

Pumpkins and painted leaves — when the weather behaves as it
should, autumn in the Rochester area is beautiful and
prolonged.

Sunsets in the country enhance the atmosphere of timelessness
peculiar to the rural landscapes of Rochester . . . scenes and
lifestyles as enduring as the city itself.

The water-pumping windmill is alive and well in southeast Minnesota. This is one of the many which sprout like alien flowers in fields and farmyards.

At the windmill's base, a more natural flower reveals the beauty
and efficiency of radial design.

Corn has long since replaced wheat as the king of crops in this
area, and sweet corn processing is a mainstay for one of
Rochester's larger industries.

Considering all the scenic, historic and recreational facets of its environs, Rochester's appeal becomes more understandable. Yet there is something else about the city — something that cannot be explained in terms of its history, the Mayo family, or its physical appearance. It is some indefinable quality apart from these that is sensed rather than seen; something which gives Rochester a warmth uncommon to most cosmopolitan surroundings.

For many it is the aura of friendliness, even welcome, that Rochester's people seem to project. This expansive and generous attitude might be accounted for by the fact that per capita income in Rochester is well above the state and national average. But for whatever reason, there is no denying that Rochester hospitality surpasses the bounds of mere professional etiquette.

For many others, a visit to Rochester is like a pilgrimage to a shrine. Countless thousands have been given hope and life, when both had been thought lost, inside the grey, marble walls of the famous clinic. And in this way have evolved emotional ties not easily set aside.

It may also be that Rochester's people, as with Minnesotans in general, are natural products of a fulfilling and satisfying environment. Some believe the sharp changes of four seasons give Minnesotans a zest for living, a feel of self worth, and an industriousness less evident in more static climes.

But Rochester's appeal may simply be that it has always, since the day George Head first entertained visitors in his log home, been a city fundamentally given to service. With the exception of a few brief interludes in its history, it has been always a prosperous city. As such, much energy has traditionally been devoted to civic improvement, to projects aimed at elevating the spirit and providing the most material comfort. Its fine schools, beautiful parks, superior hospitals, its concern for the arts — all are part of a heritage Rochester citizens have come to take for granted.

As the poet Pope says, "The proper study of Man is Man." And if any single community could be described as following this precept, it is Rochester.

Acknowledgements

The publishers of this book are grateful to the following people who helped in its production:
George Tyrrell — Olmsted County Historical Society
Ron Hunt — Mantorville artist
David Swanson — Communications Dept., Mayo Clinic

Jerry Finn — Finn's Cameras, St. Paul
Holly Wesley and Dave Wesley, Jr.
Mary E. Hanson — Kellogg, Mn.
Tom Austin – Colorhouse Inc.
Bill Brown – John Roberts Co.

Photo Index And Technical Information

FILM –

All 35 mm photographs were taken with Kodak
Kodachrome 25 ASA film except where noted.
All 2¼ × 2¼ photographs were taken with Kodak
Ektachrome 64 ASA film except where noted.